Navigating Revelation

Navigating Revelation
Charts for the Voyage

A Pedagogical Aid

EUGENE E. LEMCIO

WIPF & STOCK · Eugene, Oregon

NAVIGATING REVELATION
Charts for the Voyage: A Pedagogical Aid

Copyright © 2011 Eugene E. Lemcio. All rights reserved. Except for brief quotations in critical publications or reviews, no part of this book may be reproduced in any manner without prior written permission from the publisher. Write: Permissions, Wipf and Stock Publishers, 199 W. 8th Ave., Suite 3, Eugene, OR 97401.

Wipf & Stock
An imprint of Wipf and Stock Publishers
199 W. 8th Ave., Suite 3
Eugene, OR 97401

www.wipfandstock.com

ISBN 13: 978-1-61097-702-9

Manufactured in the U.S.A.

Contents

Preface / vii
Abbreviations / x
Definitions / xi
Charts Summary / xiii

1. Politics: Human & Divine in Daniel / 1
2. Politics: Human & Divine in Revelation / 3
3. "Son of Man" in Daniel 7: Vision & Interpretation (Ancient and Modern) / 5
4. Interpretations of Daniel 7: Summary of Main Positions / 8
5. Ironic/Paradoxical Christologies in Revelation / 9
6. Already & Not Yet: Inaugurated & Unrealized Eschatology / 11
7. Revelation & Recapitulation? / 13
8. Revelation 6 & Isaiah 13: The Shaking of the Foundations / 16
9. Revelation 6 & 7: Questions & Answers / 19
10. Revelation 7 & 14: The Lamb & the 144,000 / 21
11. Revelation 8:1–5 & 1 Kings 18:16–40 / 24
12. Revelation 8:6–12 & Exodus 7–12 / 26
13. Revelation 9: Sphinxes & "Locusts" / 28
14. Revelation 10 & Ezekiel 1–3, 5 / 32
15. Chiasmus & Particularization in Revelation 11? / 34
16. Prophets & Witnesses: OT "Backgrounds" to Revelation 11 / 35
17. Revelation 11: Priests, Prophets, Anointed Ones, & Witnesses / 38
18. Revelation 11 & 12: Two Facets of a Whole? / 40

19. Dragon/Serpent Imagery: ANE & OT (Similarities) / 41
20. Dragon/Serpent Imagery: ANE & OT (Differences) / 42
21. Dragon/Serpent Imagery: OT (Differences) / 43
22. Revelation 12 & Exodus Imagery / 45
23. Revelation 12: "Satan's" Fall in Jewish Apocalyptic / 47
24. "I saw Satan fall from Heaven" (Luke 10:18) / 49
25. Myth in Revelation 12: Similarities (Woman-Child-Dragon, War in Heaven) / 50
26. Myth in Revelation 12: Differences (Woman-Child-Dragon) / 53
27. Revelation 12: Kerygma/Gospel-in-Myth / 55
28. Revelation 12 & Matthew 1-2: Two "Christmas" Stories / 56
29. Revelation 13–14: Animal Imagery & Followers Contrasted / 58
30. Revelation 13–14: Sinners & Saints Contrasted (by Chiasmus?) / 59
31. The Beasts of Revelation 13: a Summary of Interpretive Tendencies / 60
32. Revelation 17–18: The Prostitute, Babylon, Beasts, & Kings (Their Relationships) / 62
33. Revelation 17–19: Babylon & New Jerusalem / 63
34. Revelation 17–21: History, Myth, & Eschatology / 64
35. Revelation 17, 19, 21: A Tale of Two Cities? of Two Women? / 66

Bibliography / 67

Preface

THE IMAGE OF THE church as a vessel is an ancient one. If we examine her ship's logs, it is clear that, during stormy voyages of the past two thousand years, she has had to navigate the cross currents of interpretation with instruments that have sometimes led to false sightings and dubious soundings.

For some of those sailings, numerous cartographers have drawn contradictory "maps" in an attempt to journey safely (if not directly) from the past to the present and future. Given such a checkered itinerary, what makes me regard the following as an improvement over the others? In a word, they have been the results of preconceived notions and external schemes imposed upon the changing face of the ocean that is Revelation.

Leaving aside the nautical metaphor, regarding the relation between this work and that of Mark Wilson's *Charts on the Book of Revelation: Literary, Historical, and Theological Perspectives*, this may be said: Wilson emphasizes the first two aspects of the subtitle, while my effort focuses more on the literary and interpretive. While Wilson is useful as a *reference* tool, this book is designed more specifically as a *teaching* instrument. Of course, ideally, both can be used for different aspects of a complete study. So, rather than "reinvent" even some of Wilson's "wheels," I mean to complement them.

The following charts are to be understood primarily as guides—as means, not as ends. Rather than providing a rigid structure for indoctrination and memorization, such tables (and the leading statements and questions which I have provided) should foster orderly and disciplined teaching and learning. The displays are of two kinds: one set (for example, numbers 1–7) provides data in categories that can be inferred because of their frequency or strategic nature (the subjective nature of this judgment being reduced by evidence and argument).

Interspersed among the thirty-five charts (beginning with #8 and amounting to about a third of the total) are those that demonstrate systematic analysis (a taking apart) and synthesis (a putting together) by posing "investigative" questions long used in literature and journalism classes: Who? (agent: initiator or recipient), What? (action/event), When? (time), Where? (place), How? (means/manner/method/instrument), How Far/Many/Much? (scope/quantity), What Kind? (quality), Why? (purpose/cause), So What? (significance), etc.

Using these categories enables analysis and synthesis to be *comprehensive* in that all aspects of a narrative or argument can be covered. At the same time, they make it possible for one to detect that which *integrates* the parts. Approaching literature in this way assists students to develop skills in *comparison* (noting similarities) and *contrast* (seeing differences). Applying such neutral classification helps to *increase objectivity* and to limit imposing agendas foreign to a text. No rigid sequence need be followed when employing the above. They can be freely re-ordered to achieve the greatest pedagogical effect. Finally, the selection of passages and themes is meant to be *illustrative* and *paradigmatic* so that teachers and students can use them as models in expanding the range of their own inquiries.

In comparing and contrasting John's appropriation of OT themes and images, one can observe that he did not conduct jigsaw puzzle prophecy: making pieces fit into a (predetermined?) whole. Rather, the Theologian not only ad*o*pted biblical material, he also ad*a*pted it (i.e., transformed it) according to his conception of and response to God's word and deed in Christ (both past and contemporaneous). Besides encouraging students to visualize such alterations of canonical texts, another table treats modifications of disputed Jewish literature (chart 23).

I have begun this study with the political terminology and son of man "Christology" of Daniel because this work has contributed so profoundly to the genre, terms, and themes of Revelation. Charts 1 and 2 show how extensively vocabulary for the exercise of royal authority dominates each document. Charts 3 and 4 prepare one for the more developed son of man Christology of Revelation 1, which appears as the first of several ironic/paradoxical Christologies throughout the work (chart 5).

Even though every chapter in Revelation has been touched upon, some have received more attention than others—especially chapter 12. At a crucial moment in the drama, the startling claim is made: "they [the aforementioned brothers and sisters] have conquered him [the Dragon, Serpent, Devil, Satan] by the blood of the Lamb and by the word of their testimony, for they did not cling to life, even in the face of death" (v. 11). All else tends to extend from and revolve around this affirmation.

As a means of making it available to the widest possible audience, the author similarly adopted, adapted, and arranged foundational myths of the Eastern Mediterranean and Mesopotamia according to his convictions about and experience of Jesus—both past and contemporaneous (charts 25 and 26). And clothed in this genre is an expression of the unifying kerygma of the NT itself (chart 27).

I have used the NRSV, except in those passages referring to the son of man figure in Daniel 7, Psalm 8, and in Revelation 1 and 14 (where I resort to the RSV). I did this principally because it has preserved the expression "son of man" rather than converting it to the generic "human" or "mortal." Although not a title *per se*, the term retains a certain formal quality, which NT writers exploit when they appropriate it. Such usage is obscured by the NRSV's otherwise welcome efforts to avoid gender specific translation. Because this tool is meant to engage students (and teachers!) with primary texts before they resort to secondary resources, I have avoided referring to the latter in footnotes. Works supporting direct study of primary materials are cited internally and listed in the bibliography.

To those who might view an academic approach of this kind as foreign to the spirit of Revelation's message (which has so much to do with worship of the living God and encouragement of God's people to remain loyal under the worst circumstances), I say this: St. Paul, in his exposition about the proper use of spiritual gifts in worship, insisted that praying in the Spirit needs to engage the mind; and singing in the Spirit must involve the understanding (1 Cor 14:15). Consequently, study and song belong together. It is right to ponder as well as praise. In the process, one can more deeply enter into the revealed mystery, which invites rather than forbids.

Abbreviations

ANET	*Ancient Near Eastern Texts Relating to the Old Testament*
BCE	Before the Common Era
CSEL	*Corpus scriptorum ecclesasticorum latinorum*
CT	*Christianity Today*
CE	Common Era
JSNT	*Journal for the Study of the New Testament*
JTS	*Journal of Theological Studies*
LCL	Loeb Classical Library
LXX	Septuagint of the Greek Old Testament
MT	Masoretic Text of the Hebrew Bible
NASB	New American Standard Bible
NETS	New English Translation of the Septuagint
NRSV	New Revised Standard Version
NT	New Testament
OT	Old Testament
Pss Sol	*Psalms of Solomon*
RSV	Revised Standard Version
SNTSMS	Society for New Testament Studies Monograph Series
TynBul	*Tyndale Bulletin*

Definitions

Although some of these may be contestable, I offer them so that the reader will not be in doubt about the way that they are employed in the following exercises:

1. **Chiasmus**: a pattern whose sequence is reversed mid-point in a series. The pattern may embrace a large amount of material (as in chapters 12–20*), a lesser quantity of text (See the notes on chapters 13 and 14), or as small a unit as a verse.

2. **Generalization****: a broad, encompassing statement (sometimes a conclusion) preceded by a series of particulars (or a developed argument).

3. **Metaphor**: a comparison or analogy of greater complexity than a **simile**.

4. **Myth**: a narrative, expressed in characteristic metaphors, enabling an individual or community to connect with foundational realities (origins, continuity, destiny).

6. **Particularization****: the development in greater detail of a general statement.

7. **Politics**: an understanding of power and a strategy for distributing it in human community. In the Bible, there are only two ways for doing so: human politics and divine politics.

8. **Recapitulation**: the repeated return to and extension of a theme or an image.

9. **Symbol**: literally, "a throwing together"—a figure of speech, an object, or an action that relates one to a larger reality.

*Mark Wilson shows how the following pattern organizes the second half of Revelation:

(12) **Dragon** [A], (13) **Beasts** [B], (17) **Babylon** [C]—their Rise
(18) **Babylon** [C'], (19) **Beasts** [B'], (20) **Dragon** [A']—their Demise

**Professor Robert Traina first introduced me to these (and other) categories.

Charts Summary

In general, and on the whole, all or some of the following occur in most instances. One could preface each exercise by saying a version of, "As you look at the text with the aid of the charts, identify as many as possible of the following (1) characteristics and (2) modifications/transformations":

(1) Characteristics: Revelation is (or its themes are)

    a. evangelical in content and character: the Good News trumps the Bad News

    b. political in the sense that its author is dealing with the nature of power and its distribution in community (whether that be on earth or in heaven)

    c. prophetic in that the author is "speaking truth to power" (to employ an important expression liable to becoming a cliché)

    d. primordial in origin and eschatological in consequence

    e. foundational in depth and therefore mythic in expression

    f. terrestrial in location: the New Jerusalem descends to a new earth, where God wants to dwell with humankind (21:1–7)

(2) Modifications/Transformations (largely in scope) occur from

    a. "historical" narrative to mythic narrative

    b. reporting to envisioning

    c. local to global

    d. particular to universal

    e. ethnic to multi-cultural

    f. national to international

    g. earthly to heavenly/cosmic

h. human to supernatural: both divine and demonic

i. external to internal (behind the scenes)

j. past to present and future

k. theological to christological (from God to Christ, or from God to God and God's Christ)

1

POLITICS: Human & Divine in Daniel

	1	2	3	4	5	6	7	8	9	10	11	12	Totals
Kingdom	3	10	3	11	7	7	9	1	3		6		62
King	17	43	29	15	17	26	3	5	2	4	23		184
Reign (vb.)						2	1	1					4
Authority			3	8	4	1	6						22
Power(ful)		1	2		1		1	2			3		9
Ruler	1	2	3	1						1			8
Throne			1	4			2						7
	21	56	41	39	28	35	23				32		

1. Because Daniel supplies so many of the key themes and terms in Revelation (and in the Synoptic Gospels, for that matter), I display the data and provide the following observations and questions. (They will not have to be repeated in the chart on Revelation that follows.) Although textual variants in some cases affect the numbers, they do not contradict the overwhelming preponderance of the figures above.

2. The best way to reduce (if not completely avoid) subjectivity about de-

termining a/the dominant theme of any literary work is to apply the criterion of frequency. Which terms or clusters of terms occur in most instances, at certain concentrations, and at critical junctures? This display indicates how much political terminology (both separately and collectively) covers the text.

3. As a working definition, regard politics to be an understanding of power and as a strategy for distributing it in human community. In the Bible, there are only two ways: human politics and divine politics. The latter is summarized especially by a multiple refrain at 4:17, 25, and 32: "The Most High rules human kingdoms and gives them to whom he will" and, according to v. 17b, "sets over it the lowliest of human beings." According to the LXX of 4:28(31), Daniel tells King Nabouchodonosor [Nebuchadnezzar], "The kingdom of Babylon has been taken away from you and is being given to another, a contemned [or "despised"] person in your house. Lo, I establish him over your kingdom, and he will receive your authority and your glory and your luxury so that you may recognize that the God of heaven has authority in the kingdom of humans and he will give it to whomever he desires. Now, by sunrise, another king will rejoice in your house and will take your glory and your power and your authority" (NETS).

4. The numbers represent Greek terms as they occur in the LXX, the Bible most often cited and alluded to by the writers of the NT. A comparison with Semitic and English concordances does not materially affect the quantity and distribution of the terms. All such reference works testify to the heavily political context of the writer's various themes. The sheer number and variety of instances for royal terminology is itself impressive. Can there be any doubt that dominion and rule are dominant themes in this book?

5. Regard the throne as the "seat" of power from which kings rule. In the extended chapter 4 in the LXX of Daniel, the throne imagery is increased several fold. This is more apparent in the NETS.

6. Perhaps the clearest definition of Israelite kingship (at least its ideal) is provided by Deut 17:14–20. Distinguish between negative and positive aspects of the job description. See also Psalm 72.

2

Politics: Human & Divine in Revelation

	1	2	3	4	5	6	7	8	9	10	11	12
Throne	1	1	2	14	5	1	7	1			1	1
Kingdom	2			1							1	1
King	1					1			1	1		
Reign					1						2	
Authority		1				1			4		2	1
Power	1		1	1	1		1				1	1
God Almighty	1			1							1	
Totals				16							8	

	13	14	15	16	17	18	19	20	21	22	Totals
Throne	1	1		2			2	3	2	2	47
Kingdom				1	3						9
King			1		2	8	2	4		1	22
Reign							1	2		1	7
Authority	5	1			1	2	1		1	1	21
Power	1		1		1	1	1			1	12
God Almighty				1	2			2		1	9
Totals				8		14		10			

1. Unlike in Daniel, by far most of the royal terminology is applied to God and Christ.

2. Forty-seven of the sixty-two instances (or 76 percent) of the NT's usage occur here. Why does most of the "throne" ("seat of power") terminology appear in chapter 4? Recall that the scope shifts from local and earthly in chapters 2–3 to global and cosmic in the remainder.

3. On thirty-eight occasions, some form of "king/kingdom/rule" occurs. "Authority" comes a close second.

4. Where do the main concentrations of most terms take place?

3

"Son of Man" in Daniel 7: Vision & Interpretation (Ancient & Modern)

Daniel 7: Vision	Explanation #1	Explanation #2	Explanation #3
3 Beasts (2–6)			
4th *Beast*	4 *Kings* (17)	4th *Beast* (19–20)	4th *Kingdom* (23)
10 horns			10 *Kings* (24)
11th *horn*		11th *horn*	11th *King*
*speak*ing great things (8) *speak*ing great *words* (11)			*speak*s *words* (25) against *Most High* [MH]
		made war with & conquered *SMH* (21)	wore out *SMH*
			tried changing times & law
			temporarily victorious
Ancient of Days [AD] *judges* (9–10)		AD *judges* (22)	court *judges* (26)
one like a son of man (13)	Saints Most High [SMH] (18)	SMH	People of *SMH* (27)
given dominion glory	receive	possess	given dominion
kingship	**king**dom	**king**dom	**king**dom
universal service			*universal service*
indestructible **king**ship			eternal **king**dom

5

1. Because John's lead Christology (chapter 1) is that of the "one like a son of man" (occurring again in chapter 14), and because it is derived from Daniel 7 and 10, it is necessary to examine the dynamics of the original usage.

2. The overall political emphasis displayed earlier in chart 1 lies behind its particular manifestation in this chapter, as the bold font highlights.

3. Although vv. 1–14 present the vision proper, explanations 2 and 3 also contain expansions (additional details of the original vision).

4. John J. Collins summarizes three main views about the identity of the son of man figure and the Saints/Holy Ones of the Most High: (a) a collective symbol for loyal Israel under assault, (b) a human representative of these people, and (c) an angel (Michael?) at the head of a band of angels—both being the heavenly patrons of God's earthly people. See chart 4 for a fuller treatment.

5. Although the MT enables one to read v. 27—and (c)—in this manner, the LXX prevents one from doing so for two reasons: angels are never referred to as "holy"; and v. 27 speaks of "the holy people of the Most High" rather than "the people of the Saints/Holy Ones of the Most High" (MT).

6. I have argued in *TB* that we will be distracted from the central point by focusing on the figure's *identity* (one of the above). Rather, the stress should be on the nature of his *human-like condition*—regardless of who he is/represents: an embattled but loyal Israel, its lowly human representative, or a vulnerable member of the angelic order (or one from the lower ranks). For the sake of argument, work with "son of man" as an idiom for humanity in its frailty and vulnerability—the downside of human experience. See Bowker, Burkett, and Lemcio.

7. And one needs to give close attention to the dynamic aspects of the mini-drama (narrative *in nuce*) taking place (rather than focusing on the *denoument*): a kingdom was granted to one who had previously had none; glory was given to him who had been without it; authority was bestowed upon a "personage" who had lacked it.

8. This phenomenon belongs to the widespread biblical theme of reversal: God raises the lowly and brings down the high and mighty. (See for example, the Song of Hannah in 1 Sam 2:1–10 and the Song of Mary

in Luke 1:51–53.) Daniel and Revelation (and the Synoptic Gospels, for that matter) underscore the primarily political nature of that reversal, as the frequent terminology abundantly illustrates. At issue is, who rules (really) and how?

4

Interpretations of Daniel 7: Summary of Main Positions

	1	2	3
"[one] like a son of man" (vv. 13–14)	*collective* symbol Only: --suffering of a "frail human" --exalted, empowered in the vision Only	*individual* human (the Messiah?) --No suffering --exalted, empowered in heaven	angel (Michael?) --No suffering --exalted, empowered in heaven
"saints of the Most High" (vv. 15–27)	God's holy people --loyal --embattled by kings (=beasts) --to be exalted, empowered on earth	God's holy people --loyal --embattled by kings (=beasts) --to be exalted, empowered on earth	God's holy angels --loyal --embattled by demonic "beasts" --to be exalted, empowered in heaven --parallel holy, loyalists embattled by kings on earth

1. C. F. D. Moule is a representative of those holding number 1.

2. Representative of the inclination to blend all three (inferring a divine-human figure who is exalted after suffering) is Seyoon Kim.

3. John J. Collins (whose summary I have elaborated upon) and Christopher Rowland are supporters of view 3.

4. I do not so much focus on the *identity* of the figure as I stress the *nature* of the humanity with whom the figure is being compared—its frailty, vulnerability.

5

Ironic/Paradoxical Christologies in Revelation

(1)	(2)	(3)	(4)	(5)
1:13–16	5:5–6	12:4–5, 11	14:14–16	19:11–16
A. Son of Man	B. Lion, Tribe, Judah	A. Newborn Child	A. Son of Man	B. King of Kings, Lord of Lords
B.' Double-edged sword		A.' Blood of Lamb	B.' crowned, cloud-borne	B.' Double-edged sword
B. Ancient of Days / Angel	A. Slaughtered Lamb	B. Rule the Nations	A.' Ordered by Angel	A. Bloody Robe
A.' From the mouth		B.' Conquered Dragon	B. From Temple (of God)	A.' From the mouth

1. See chart 3 displaying the setting of this term in Daniel 7. In his comprehensive survey of the expression, Delbert Burkett (13–21, especially 14–17) discusses an interpretation going back at least five hundred years: "son of man" as an idiom for the downside of human experience: its frailty and vulnerability. In recent years, the most comprehensive defense of this rendering is by John Bowker. I have argued for it in the Old Greek of Daniel. Whether or not you agree with this definition, regard it (for the sake of argument) as the first of five presentations of an ironic or paradoxical Christology in Revelation.

2. The irony or paradox lies in that an image of weakness (A., A.') is joined to one of strength (B., B.'). Is the message: strong, although weak; strength through weakness, etc.? Whichever of the two dimensions occurs first is determined by the dramatic effect desired. The powerful aspect of the son of man image in column 1 is doubled in that his glorious features appeared to be derived both from those of the Ancient of

Days in Dan 7:9–10 and those of a magnificent (angelic?) being, human in appearance (10:5–6).

3. What do the frequency and distribution of this Christology suggest? Relate it to the data displayed in charts 1 and 2 regarding the prominence of politics—the nature and distribution of both divine and human power.

4. What difference does it make that the double-edged sword in the case of the son of man (column 1) and Word of God (column 5) issues from their mouth rather than being wielded by their hands? Why is the location of symbols significant?

5. What are the features of conventional power conveyed by "the Lion of the Tribe of Judah and the Root of David" (column 2)? What characteristics of unconventional power are conveyed by the Lamb-as-slaughtered? How is "conquering" to be understood by Christian readers?

6. Chapter 12 (column 3) contains other ironies (made even more vivid by the view of females in the ancient world): a *woman* vs. a great red dragon; a *pregnant* woman vs. a great red dragon; a pregnant woman in the *final stages of labor* vs. a great red dragon; a *newborn child* vs. a great red dragon. Is there any doubt about who will win? Can a bloodied Lamb conquer the large and fearsome Dragon (v. 11)—who, by definition, is also Satan, the Devil, and that Ancient Serpent (v. 9)?

7. Could the dynamics of chapter 14 (column 4, A and B') reflect the "Christology" of Psalm 8 regarding the son of man (RSV): "thou hast made him less than God, and dost crown him with glory and honor" (v. 5)? Prof. Francis Wilson has observed to me that this awkward detail, that the crowned and cloud-borne figure takes orders from an angel, may reflect the LXX wording of the Psalm, which the author of Hebrews quotes at 2:7—"Thou didst make him ["them," NRSV] for a little while lower than the angels, thou hast crowned him with glory and honor . . .".

8. The point is made twice (at both the beginning and end of the book) that the conflict is a war of words—unconventional warfare. Why is this significant for the interpretation of Revelation? Does it square with the fact that John provides no actual description of a battle scene: where armies clash—including that of the so-called "Battle of Armageddon"? What is the real name of the battle according to 16:14?

6

Already & Not Yet: Inaugurated & Unrealized Eschatology

	Already (Local: in the Churches)	Not Yet (Local: in the Churches)	Not Yet (Global & Unconditional)
Tribulation	"share with you . . . the t. and the kingdom" (1:9)	"for ten days you will have tribulation" (2:10)	
	"I know your tribulation and your poverty" (2:9)	"will throw her [with them] into great t." (2:22)	
		(conditional)	
	"those who *are* com*ing* out of the great t." (7:14)		
Coming		"I will come to you [soon]" (2:5, 16)	"the hour of trial which is coming on the whole world" (3:10)
		(conditional)	
			"I am coming soon" (3:11; 22:7, 12, 20)

1. In some English translations (including the NRSV), "tribulation" is rendered by other expressions, thereby obscuring the word's presence in contexts where it refers to a condition contemporaneous with the author and original readers. At these points, I have employed the RSV. The Greek means "pressure" or "squeeze."

2. At 7:14, the continuous action in the present (which in the Greek is clear) is hidden in most modern translations. The RSV and NIV say, "have come out"; the AV (KJV): "which came out"; the NEB: "who have passed through"—none of which conveys the sense of the original. The NASB comes closest with "who come out." What difference do these renderings make regarding one's understanding of the tribulation?

3. "The [worldwide] hour of testing" (3:10) seems to be referring to a separate event since a different Greek word is used.

4. How are local, conditional experiences of tribulation and Jesus' coming related to the global, unconditional ones?

7

Revelation & Recapitulation?

	6	11	12	13	16
1.		beast arising from abyss (7)		beast arising from sea (1)	
2.		will **make war** on witnesses		to **make war** on saints (7)	
3.		--& conquer them		--& conquer them	
4.	great **earth-quake** (12)	great earthquake (13)			violent **earth-quake** (18)
5.	every island removed				every island fled (20)
6.	every **mountain** removed (14)				**mountain**s not found
7.		10th of **city** fell			great **city** split (19)
8.					cities of nations fell
9.		**great** city: Sodom & Egypt (8)			**Great** Babylon remembered
10.	the great **day** (17)				the great **day** of
11.	(**God's** & the Lamb's)				**God** the Almighty (14)
12.		where Lord crucified	blood of the Lamb (11)		
13.		**loud voices in heaven** (15)	**loud voice in heaven** (10)		**loud voices** (17)

6	11	12	13	16
14.	has become	have come		
15.	kingdom of our Lord	kingdom of our God		
16.	and of his Messiah	and of his Messiah		
17.	will reign forever	son/male child to rule (5)		
18.	kingdom of the world	all nations		
19.	2 witnesses up to heaven (12)	son/male child taken to God		
20. of their **wrath** 21. **has come**	your **wrath** **has come** (18)			

1. Might chapter 13's expansion of the first beast's arising from the sea (line 1) be an example of particularizing the brief statement in chapter 11 about the (single) beast's rising [continuing action in the Greek] from the abyss (deepest part of the ocean)? In each instance, the account of his assaulting God's people (or their representatives) is rendered in identical language (lines 2–3).

2. Which two previous chapters does chapter 16 seem to incorporate?

3. How is it possible for the author in chapter 16 to make such claims about islands and mountains (lines 5–6), when they had undergone similar radical movement, ten and five chapters earlier? Is it possible for three endings to occur—unless one is dealing with something other than chronological, linear ordering? Also, keep in mind the comparison of chapter 6 with Isaiah 13 in chart 8.

4. How is it that the foundational recital (the beginning of the Christian narrative) occurs at chapter 12—in the middle of the book? (See the separate treatments of chapter 12 in charts 22–25.) Obviously, the author is not bound to a chronological or linear sequencing of the material. Various patterns and strategies are at work, as we have repeatedly seen.

5. Would it be possible to regard chapters 11 and 12 as the flip sides of a larger reality? What is emphasized in each? (See the fuller treatment in chart 18.)

6. Reflect on the references to "day" in both cases (line 9). Might this mean that chapter 16 is an expansion of themes in chapter 6? Note the actual name of the battle in 16:14. Is it the "Battle of Armageddon"? Does John describe the battle *per se*? Could the point be that evil forces are no match for divine power, once it is unleashed—that the conflict is not worth recounting (much less waging), only the results?

8

Revelation 6 & Isaiah 13: The Shaking of the Foundations

	Isaiah 13	Revelation 6
What?	anger/**wrath** (3, 13): **day of** the Lord (6, 9)	**wrath** (16–17): great **day of** God & Lamb
Why?	against evil, pride, arrogance, insolence (11)	[shame] inability to stand in their presence (16–17)
From Whom?	Lord of hosts & consecrated ones & warriors (3–4, 13)	God & Lamb (16–17)
Against Whom?	Babylon (1, 19)	kings, magnates, generals, rich, powerful, slave & free (15)
By Whom?	Medes, king(dom)s, nations (4, 17–18)	[God & Lamb]
How (1)?	conventional warfare (4, 15–18)	Lamb's opening 6th Seal (12)
How (2)? [Note placement: between 1 & 19: the historical references to Babylon]	**stars** & their constellations not give light (10) **sun** dark… **moon** not shed light **heavens** tremble (13) **earth** shaken	**stars** fell to earth (13) **sun** black as sackcloth (12) **moon** like blood **heavens**/sky vanished like a scroll rolling (14) every island & mountain removed great *earth*quake (12)
Where? (Place)	the land & earth (5), [Middle East] (12, 17, 19–20)	entire earth (13, 15)
How far? (Scope)	local, particular	global, universal
When? (Time)	past (from our pov)	past (Wall: Jesus event)
	future (near): "close at hand" (22)	"future": (near/indeterminate)
	historical [Medes conquered Babylon]	eschatological

16

1. The list of identical words ("stars," "sun," "moon," "heavens," and "earth") in Isa 13:10 and Rev 6:13–14 and the use of similar terms ("dark" . . . "black" and "shaken" . . . "quake") suggests that St. John had this passage in mind. From Isa 34:4 comes the language of skies rolling like a scroll (6:14).

2. The same five items, though in different order, occur in Luke 21:25–26 in direct connection with the fall of Jerusalem (v. 24). In keeping with Isaiah, Luke's Jesus has historicized the eschatological phenomenon. Cosmic collapse had not occurred during Babylon's capture by the Medes (vv. 1, 17, 19, 22) several centuries before; nor did it do so with the Roman victory over the Jewish defenders in 70 CE. These phenomena lead one to ask, "Even though the scope of John's vision was wider than that of his predecessors, might the language be just as metaphorical?" The message seems to be, "You cannot win; your doom is assured; the elements of the universe itself are fighting against you!" If that be so, should the natural world be seen as a target of divine wrath or its instrument? The latter seems to be the better conclusion, especially since the "destroyers of the earth" are themselves to be destroyed (11:18).

3. Therefore, is it legitimate to regard these as "signs of the times" preceding the end of existence as we know it? How many of the phenomena are predictable according to astronomical, geological, and meteorological conditions? How much does continuous global communication convey the sense that they are on the increase and more widespread? Should all this not mean rather that the Theologian belonged to "the goodly company of the prophets" who adapted a common stock of vocabulary to their particular circumstances?

4. Regarding the **What?** (action/event), see the similarity of language concerning "wrath" and "Day" (Isa 13:3, 6, 9, 13 and Rev 6:16–17).

5. However, from this point on, the likeness stops, as shown by a look at the source of wrath (**From Whom?**). What was originally from the "Lord Almighty and the Holy Ones" (13:3–4, 13) is now from God and the Lamb (6:16–17). A Christological factor has been added to the existing and ongoing theological one.

6. Furthermore, the means (**How?**) differ significantly, too, from conventional warfare by human agents to unconventional "warfare" by the Lamb's "merely" opening of the 6th seal.

7. The target of wrath (**Against Whom?**) is varied, too—as are **Place and Scope**: In the case of Isaiah 13, it is Babylon (vv. 1, 19, 22), the **Place** being the this-worldly lands of the Middle East (vv. 5, 11) and the **Scope** local (vv. 12, 17, 19–20). With regard to Revelation, the objects of wrath are the politically great, rich, and powerful, both free and slave (v. 15) throughout the entire earth (vv. 13, 15): in other words, both global and universal—but still terrestrial.

8. Closely related to place is **Time (When?)**: from our point of view, the action of Isaiah 13 took place in the past (though from the prophet's point of view, the events were to take place in the near future: sooner rather than later). Although some interpreters take Revelation 6 to be imbedded in the Jesus event, others view them as occurring in the progressively unfolding future—i.e., as ongoing eschatological events.

9

Revelation 6 & 7: Questions & Answers

6:1–8	7:1
The First Four Seals	Introduction to the Sealed of Israel
1. **Four** Living Creatures	1. **Four** Angels (four living creatures [v. 11])
2. **Four** Horsemen	2. **Four** Corners of the Earth
3. **Four** Seals	3. **Four** Winds
4. **Fourth** of the Earth	
6:9–11	7:4–8
The Fifth *Seal* (Martyrs)	The *Sealed* of Israel
1. Those slain for the Word of God & testimony given	
2. **Question #1**: "How long?"	2.
Question answered: When **number of** fellow servants & brothers & sisters to be killed is completed	**number of** servants of God sealed (v. 3)
3. [Implied **Question #2**: "How many?"]	3. [Implied **Answer**]: 144,000 (v. 4 and cf. 14:1, 3)
6:15–17	7:9–17
The Sixth Seal (and a Vast Crowd)	A Great Multitude

6:1–8	7:1
1. People of every rank, wealth, and class	1. innumerable, multi-lingual, international persons
2. Question #3: "Who is able to **stand**?"	2. Answer: "standing" (9)
[before] "the one seated on the **throne** and from the wrath of the **Lamb**"	"before the **throne** & before the **Lamb**"
	"the ones who have come out [lit. "are coming"] out of the great ordeal" ["tribulation"]
	who "have washed their robes . . . in the blood of the Lamb" (14)

1. I have adopted and adapted a display originally created many years ago by a now-unknown former student, "Mark," whose family name escapes me. It illustrates how a perspective introduced by the teacher can be applied and extended by the pupil—and then be appropriated later by the teacher (with gratitude).

2. The presence of the seven terms in both chapters requires attention: "four," "seal," "number," "servants," "stand," "throne," and "Lamb." Furthermore, references to a smaller group within a larger one in both instances also merit consideration.

3. Then there is the phenomenon of three questions being asked (one of them implied) in chapter 6, which receive answers in chapter 7.

4. While the dynamics of 6:9–11 and 7:4–8 are equivalents, those in 6:15–17 and 7:9–17 are opposites.

5. Consequently, do we have here an instance where adjoining chapters are the flip side of a larger whole? If so, it would be another reason for avoiding a non-linear reading of the material.

10

Revelation 7 & 14: The Lamb & the 144,000

Revelation 7	Revelation 14
3) servants of God marked with seals on **foreheads**	1) **Lamb's** & Father's name on **foreheads** (Cf. below.)
4) **144,000** sealed (4x) from all tribes of Israel	**144,000** standing on Mt. Zion
	3) before <u>throne</u> (see below)
	elders & 4 living creatures
	144K redeemed from earth (Cf. v. 4.)
	4) follow **Lamb** wherever he goes (Cf. below.)
	12) keep commands of God & hold fast faith of Jesus
	13) die in the Lord
	deeds follow
	will rest
9) great multitude before <u>throne</u> & **Lamb**	3) before <u>throne</u>
10) salvation to God on <u>throne</u> & to **Lamb**	
11) around the <u>throne</u>: *elders, 4 living creatures*	*elders & 4 living creatures*
14) Are com*ing** out of the great ordeal [Tribulation]	

21

Revelation 7	Revelation 14
washed white in blood of **Lamb**	
15) before God's <u>throne</u>	3) before <u>throne</u>
worship day & night in temple	
the one on the <u>throne</u> will shelter them	
16) never thirsty or harmed	
17) **Lamb** at center of <u>throne</u>	1) **Lamb's** & Father's name on **foreheads**
will shepherd & guide	4) follow **Lamb** wherever he goes
God will wipe away every tear	
A. 144K General	A' 144K Specific
1. Sealed (6x) for protection	1. named for identification
2. identified by tribe	2. engaged in following
B. Great Multitude (Specific)	
1. rewarded with <u>throne</u> appearance	
2. engaged in worship	
C. support the view of a "vanguard" or "a few good men & women"	symbolized & universalized

*For this translation, see #2 in chart 6.

1. Since references to the 144,000 occur only in chapters 7 and 14 (and because their identity in chapter 7 is so disputed), it is important to compare and contrast them.

2. The other important term shared by both is "Lamb."

3. Yet, the Lamb references in chapter 7 occur with the "vast multitude" rather than with the 144,000. In chapter 14, they all appear only in connection with the 144,000.

4. However, "throne," "elder," and "living creature" terminology is applied both to the great multitude of chapter 7 and the 144,000 of chapter 14.

5. At least, this much can be said: the 144,000 of chapter 7 are sealed for *protection*; in chapter 7, they are named for *identification*.

6. Chapter 7 is concerned with worship and reward; chapter 14 seems to indicate the life of following, suffering, and dying that led to reward and worship.

7. Discuss the merits of this analogy: although the entire nation was to function as a "nation/kingdom of priests" (Exod 19:6), nevertheless, it was the tribe of Levi (only one of the twelve) that supplied candidates for a priestly class within it. Likewise, the role of "a few good men and women" (chapter 7) becomes the assignment for all (chapter 14).

Israel as a whole: a *nation* of **priests**	144,000: an uncountable *multitude*
Levi: a *tribe* of **priests**	144,000: from 12 tribes of *Israel*

11

Revelation 8:1–5 & 1 Kings 18:16–40

	1 Kgs 18:16–40	Rev 8:1–5 (7th Seal)
1. Genre (Form?)	Narrative	Apocalyptic Symbolic Narrative
2. What? (Action)	Judgment: transform? punish?	Judgment: transform? punish?
3. From Whom? (Source)	God	God
4. By Whom? (Agent)	Elijah	(8th) Angel + all the saints
5. How (1)? (Means)	prayer	prayers + smoke of incense
6. How (2)? (Means)	fire from God	fire from heaven via Angel
7. Against Whom? (Target)	(priests of) Baal	[God's enemies ("earth dwellers")]
8. For Whom? (Beneficiary)	the holy remnant	[the saints]
9. Why/So what? (Point)	God rules, not Baal	[God rules]
	Israel to resume allegiance	[demonstration?]
10. Where? (Place)	N. Kingdom of Israel	heaven & earth
	Palestine, Middle East	
11. How much/far? (Scope)	local	global
	"ethnic"	international
	particular	universal
	earthly	cosmic
12. When? (Time)	historical	eschatological: before Jesus' return
	past	future (the last days)

1. Matters of religion and politics are intertwined, the former being used to legitimate the latter.

2. During the confrontation at Mt. Carmel, Elijah sought to turn his people back to the worship of Yahweh by convincing them (and the god's priests) that Baal (literally "Lord") was false.

3. What does the prophet's success imply about the rule of Ahab and Jezebel? Does John imply this regarding the gods of subsequent "caesars" and their reigns? Is this to be the nature of the final confrontation, too?

12

Revelation 8:6–12 & Exodus 7–12

	Exodus 7–12	Rev 8:6–12 (4 Trumpets)
1. Genre (Form)	Narrative	Apocalyptic Symbolic Narrative
2. What? (Action)	Judgment: transform? punish?	Judgment: transform? / punish?
3. From Whom? (Source)	God	God
4. By Whom? (Agent)	Moses, Destroying Angel	4 angels
5. Against Whom? (Target)	Pharaoh, Egypt	non-animate & animate life
6. For Whom? (Beneficiary)	enslaved Israel	[God's people]
7. How? (Means, Method)	10 plagues	4 Trumpets
8. Why? / So What? (Point)	God sovereign,	[save earth dwellers? Cf. 9:20–21, 16:9, 11.]
	free Israel	
9. Where? (Place)	Egypt	heavens & earth
10. How Much / Far? (Scope)	local	global (but limited: 1/3)
	ethnic	international (but limited: 1/3)
	particular	universal (but limited: 1/3)
	earthly	cosmic
11. When? (time)	historical	eschatological (before Jesus' return)
	past	future, last days

1. Similar issues are at stake in this section and its OT background as in Rev 8:1–5 (chart 11).

2. Cite the political and economic dimensions of the freedom achieved by the Exodus.

3. What did Moses' confrontation with both the wizards and pharaoh of Egypt imply about the relationship between religion, politics, and economics?

4. Is God's judgment (whether against his own people or others) always punitive? Is there an expressed (or at least implied) possibility for transformation? Is restraint being shown here? See also the purpose of the poundings given in 9:20–21 and 16:9, 11 (the throne of the beast—the seat of the Evil Empire!).

13

Revelation 9: Sphinxes & "Locusts"

Hittite Sphinx (Carchemish, 11th–9th c. BCE)	"Locusts" in Revelation 9:7–11	Egyptian Sphinx (117–138 CE) or a century earlier
1. conical crown (Upper Egypt & Elsewhere)	"like crowns of gold" (7)	head-dress, disc & horns of Isis
2. human face	"faces like human faces"	female human face
3. long braid	"hair like women's hair" (8)	curly hair topped with (See 1 & 2 above.)
4. lion's face and teeth	"teeth like lions' teeth"	crocodile's face and teeth
5. breastplates and grieves on front paws	"scales like iron breastplates" (9)	chains on torso (holding wings?)
6. wing	"noise of their wings"	pair of wings
7. tail *with face of a bird* [other similar figures have segmented scorpion's tail]	"tails like scorpions" (10)	tail ending with cobra head
8. slab at base of Roman temple to Helios-Apollo	"their king called… Apollyon" (11)	
9. Carchemish on the River Euphrates	"the great river Euphrates" (14)	

1. No one disputes the lack of resemblance between the locusts of Revelation 9 and insects of the natural world. So, the question persists, "With what can they be compared?" I first suspected a relationship between sphinx and "locust" over twenty-five years ago while flipping through an ancient Near Eastern coloring book (Conkle) in the village of Langley, WA. It seemed more than coincidental that six of seven features in the figure of a Hittite sphinx and the creatures envisioned in Revelation 9 should correspond. (The seventh exception later received an explanation.) A photo of the original image may be accessed on-line: http://www.flickr.com/photos/efendi/10175411/in/photostream/. (The drawing appears below.) That Carchemish sat on the banks of the Euphra-

tes, mentioned at v. 14 in Rev 9 (and at 16:12) increased the possibility of some connection. (The fact that, according to biblical narratives, a crucial battle in the Middle East had been fought at Carchemish involving Egypt, Babylon, and Judah (2 Chr 35:20, Jer 46:2, and Isa 10:9) enhanced its potential as the site for an apocalypticist's vision of global and eschatological conflict.)

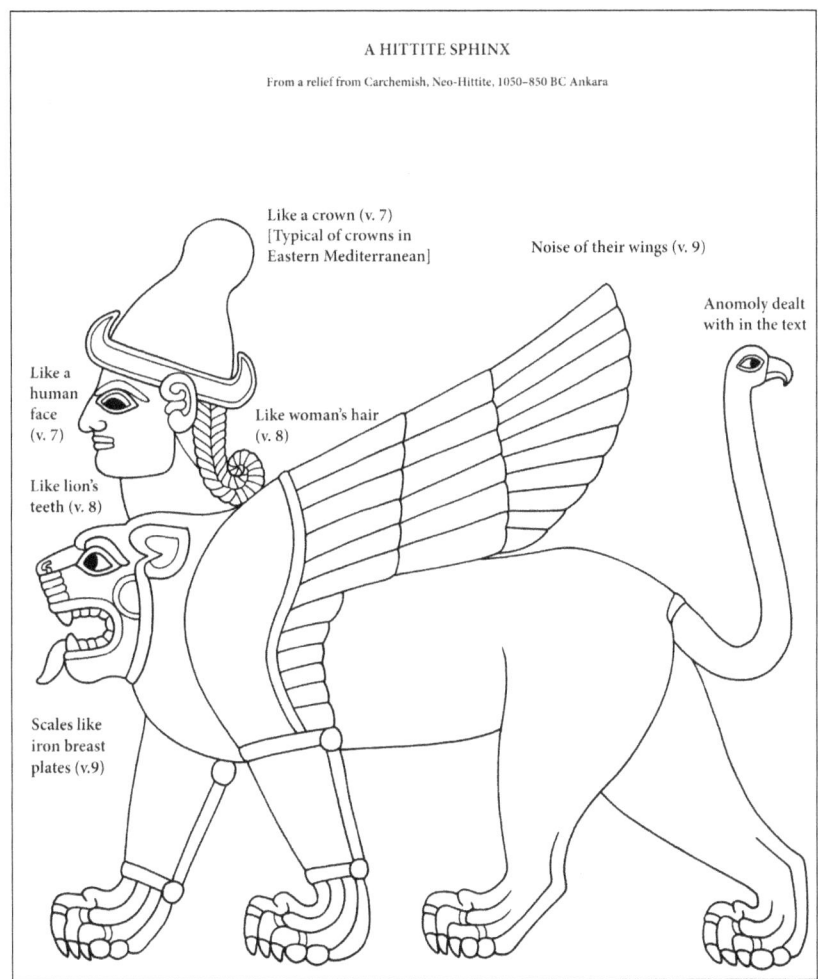

2. In an effort to bridge the gap between a child's coloring book and a scholarly explanation, I investigated the reports of excavations at Carchemish conducted by Hogarth and Woolley. The slab on which the two-dimensional figure had been carved (Hogarth, Pl. B 14a) had

been displaced by Roman constructions (perhaps of the second and third centuries CE). These included a "large and imposing temple," probably to the sun god (Woolley, 206–09). Originally, the relief in question had belonged to a panel of creatures positioned along "The Herald's Wall" (Woolley, 189) depicting mythological scenes leading to the King's Gate. From this point, "historical" ones predominate (Woolley, 191)—thereby implying a religious foundation to royal authority. Some of the supernatural figures bear both crowns (of a conical shape) and segmented scorpions' tails (Woolley, 186), the only feature lacking in the sphinx. But visionary experiences often blend images or aspects of them.

3. Requiring an answer was the question, "Would John and his readers have had access to such imagery during the first century in Roman Asia?" In other words, how could a Hittite sphinx from the 11th–9th century BCE have informed the imagination of a first-century CE author and his audience one thousand miles away? These questions were answered by the discovery that sphinx images had appeared across millennia in Mesopotamia and the Eastern Mediterranean down through the second century CE on monuments, figurines, vases, and coins. The most comprehensive study (by A. Dessenne) lists 345 hand-drawn variations on the theme (plus numerous sub-variants), this example corresponding to #226 on plate xviii. Given the appearance of such imagery on metal currency at least through the second century CE (my own numismatic research, and Hassan, 112), John's readers would have been familiar with it.

4. Therefore, wherever one looked, the long-standing double message had been maintained into the Christian era: the powers that be are upheld by the supernatural world. The underpinning of Roman rule in Egypt during the times of Trajan and Hadrian (and earlier?) by the Isis-Horus myth is reflected in the chart by features from a composite sphinx on a base relief now in Cairo (Hassan, p. 112, figure 27 and below). In addition to the features tabulated above, protruding from the lion's rump is a hawk's head crowned with solar disk and ram's horns. The wedding of gods and country goes back a long way. (Because the lion's paws are trampling on a cobra, might there be a reflection of the serpent/dragon vs. woman-child myth discussed in notes for backgrounds to Revelation 12, p. 50 [chart 25]?)

5. As with chapter 12, John employed images from his religio-political world to make both an apposite and opposite point: these creatures, far from exercising their own authority upon the earth, have been confined to the bottomless pit (literally "the abyss")—from which they have been released and authorized by an angel and star to do God's bidding: to spare vegetation while torturing unsealed humans for a limited time of five months (vv. 1–6). However, was the goal of using divine power to judge (at least in this instance and in 16:10-11) punitive or transformative (vv. 20–21)? Finally, might those who claim the Bible to be divinely inspired view the process, on some occasions, as a quickening of images already available to the conscious or present in the sub-conscious—not only stimulating *what* to adopt but *how* to adapt it? (See also chart 26.)

6. Every reasonable effort has been made by the author to trace copyright holders of the two drawings included in this section. If this has been the result of faulty communications, the publishers would be glad to hear from them.

14

Revelation 10 & Ezekiel 1–3, 5

	Ezekiel 1–3, 5	Revelation 10
1. Genre (Form)	Theophany/vision	Apocalyptic Visionary Symbolism
2. What? (Action)	eating a sweet scroll (3:1–3)	eating a bitter & sour little scroll (2, 9–10)
		prophesy (11)
3. from Whom? (Source)	Enthroned Yahweh (chapter 1)	Creator of heaven, earth, sea (6)
	accompanied by 4 "animals"	a mighty angel: sea & land, heaven & earth
	face of a lion	physical features (1), shout, lion roar, 7 thunders (2–3)
4. by Whom? (Agent)	Ezekiel (prophet) —addressed as "son of man"	[John of Patmos (prophet) —addressed by Son of Man (chapter 1)]
5. against Whom? (Target)	Exiled Judah: "House of Israel" (the unrighteous in)	many peoples, nations, languages, kings (11)
6. for Whom? (Beneficiary)	Exiled Judah (the righteous in)	many peoples, nations, languages, kings (11)
		[churches listening in: warn, encourage?]
7. How? (Means, Method)	direct encounter	mediated encounter: voice, angel
8. Why/So What? (Point)	repentance for restoration	fulfill mystery "good newsed" to prophets (7)
		[disclosed to Daniel & Isaiah: **God reigns**]

	Ezekiel 1-3, 5	Revelation 10
9. Where? (Place)	Babylon	everywhere [exiled in "Babylon"]
10. How Much/ Far? (Scope)	local	global: sea & land (1) [See 13:1, 11.]
	ethnic	international
	particular	universal
	earthly	Cosmic (4x): heaven & earth (1-2, 5-6, 8)
11. When? (Time)	historical	eschatological (before Jesus' return)
	past	future, "last" days
		no more delay (6), in the days of the 7th angel's trumpet (7)

1. Relate the (lateral) stance of the angel to the scope of the beasts' origins (13:1 and 11).

2. Relate this to the vertical dimension of his position.

3. Connect the theology of God as creator (10:6) to the mystery revealed to the prophets (v. 7). What was the message that the prophet had attempted to communicate to Nebuchadnezzar in Daniel 2 and 4? How did Isaiah define the good news (52:7)? Does this correspond to the final list of entities to be addressed: to kings (v. 11)?

4. Although extending the scope has been a regular feature by which John has transformed his scriptural sources, has it been done more extensively here—at least thus far?

15

Chiasmus & Particularization in Revelation 11?

A					A'
Temple measured					Temple opened
(1)	B			B'	(19)
	Worshipers measured			Worshipers' song recorded	
	(1)	C	C'	(15-18)	
		Witnesses to Prophesy	Witnesses Prophesy		
		(3)	(4-13)		

16

Prophets & Witnesses: OT "Backgrounds" to Revelation 11

1	2	3	4	5	6	7	Revelation 11
Law	Prophets	Priest & King	roles	place	character	Israel's Mission	2 Witnesses-Prophets
Exodus 7–12	1 – 2 Kings	Zechariah 3 & 4		temple	religious	(priestly	
Moses	Elijah	Joshua	priest	throne	political	kingdom)	
Aaron	Elisha	Zerubbabel	governor			(Exod 19:6)	
		(of Davidic descent)					
blood	sky	"2 olive trees"	fuel oil				"2 olive trees"
plagues	rain	"2 lamp stands"	vessels				"2 lamp stands"
		both "sons of oil" [dual "messiahship"?]					
		"stand before the Lord of the whole earth" (4)					"stand before the Lord of all the earth" (4)
							Churches (1:20)?
							—Smyrna (2:7–10)?
			restore Temple (Ezekiel's prophecy)	Jerusalem			—Philadelphia (3:8–12)?
Egypt	N. Kingdom	post-Exile (from Babylon)					

1. Chiasmus brings structure to the material in chapter 11. If the point of convergence, the vortex, is the place of emphasis, then what subject is at the heart of chapter 11? Of course, such a conclusion could also have been reached by tracking the location and quantity of text devoted to a single subject.

2. But there is another phenomenon occurring. The rather abbreviated themes in vv. 1–3 are expanded and specified in the remaining verses (4–19). In other words, we have here the technique of particularization.

3. The roles of prophet, king, and priest might be distinguished broadly in this manner: the prophet conveys the **Word** of God; the king executes the **Work** of God; the priest leads the people in the **Worship** of God. Via these three, the circle of revelation is completed. See also the above display (chart 16) for the transformations described below.

4. Although Zechariah 3 and 4 contribute most of the images to the identification of both witnesses (note the bold expressions in column 3), Exodus and 1–2 Kings provide their notable share of imagery as to the identity and activity of this "dynamic duo." Altogether, they embrace several significant partnerships that have contributed to the panorama of Israel's story from exodus to exile and to restoration. That narrative starts in Egypt, extends through the divided monarchy, and ends with Judah at home but not in charge.

5. Identify the political and priestly dimension that characterizes the mission of each pair:

   a. This is most clear in columns 3–7. Although the prophet Haggai focuses upon the Zerubbabel the Davidite, according to Zechariah, God calls both the high priest Joshua (3) and Zerubbabel (4) "sons of oil" (4:14)—at least a quasi-messianic expression characterized by a dual role. This allows one to examine similar dynamics in columns 1 and 2.

   b. Moses and Aaron invoke the plagues of fire and blood (column 1) because the recalcitrant king of Egypt would not let God's people go. Losing the low overhead labor costs would wreck the Egyptian economy and make it vulnerable politically. The brothers stem from Levi (Exod 2:1), the younger of them originating the Aaronic priesthood (Exod 28:1). Yahweh had commissioned Moses at the burning bush to lead the liberated Israelites to the desert for the purposes of worship (Exod 4:22).

 c. Elijah and Elisha, in their uncompromising "Yahweh alone" stance, set them (at different times), directly against king Ahab of Israel and Queen Jezebel of Sidon. The compressed narrative of Revelation 11 blends aspects of both careers, so far as miracle working is concerned. On Mt. Carmel, Elijah functioned as priest when igniting the altar dedicated to the true God of Israel (1 Kings 17–18. Cf. 2 Kings 1 and 13.).

6. How is the combined religious and political assignment articulated for the people of Israel at Exod 19:6? This same dual role is to characterize the people of God in Revelation (1:6, 5:10, and 20:6).

7. How is this seen in the positive ideals set for the king of Israel (Deut 17:14–20)?

8. How does the pairing of Ezra (priest) and Nehemiah (governor) in the restoration of city and temple continue this duality? Recall that a city represented the fundamental political unit of the ancient world. This is reflected in that "Washington," "London," "Nairobi," "Tokyo," and "Caracas" stand for the entire countries or their governments.

9. Is it any wonder that city and temple figure prominently at the opening and closing of chapter 11, along with the two prophetic witnesses?

10. So far as their identity is concerned, both individual and collective interpretations have been proposed. Of the latter, perhaps the consistent focus on pairs may provide a clue. One option is that they represent the two churches (all seven being called "lampstands" [1:20]) which, of the seven, are given a clean bill of health: Smyrna (2:7–10) and Philadelphia (3:8–12). The theme of being dead and coming alive (referring both to Jesus and to the church at Smyrna) suits the experience of the two prophets. At Philadelphia, both the royal (v. 7) and priestly emphases regarding temple and city (v. 12) also square with the consistent witness of the OT pairs.

11. With its mention of the death of Jesus (v. 9) and the more prominent expression of witness-bearing, as well as the coming of the Kingdom (vv. 15–17), might chapter 11 be another facet of the phenomena of chapter 12, with its own emphasis on the kingdom's coming (v. 10), on the blood of the Lamb (v. 11), and on the testimony borne by the woman's other children (v. 17)?

17

Revelation 11: Priests, Prophets, Anointed Ones, & Witnesses

	Exodus, 1–2 Kings, Ezekiel, Zechariah	Revelation 11
1. Genre (Form)	"Historical" Narrative	Apocalyptic Visionary Narrative
2. What? (Action)	prophetic activity & vision	witness & prophecy performed
	Ezekiel's vision of eschatological Jerusalem: **Temple & City** rebuilt	**Temple & City** *measured & opened*, God's Kingdom (& Christ's) dominates world kingdoms
3. from Whom? (Source)	God	"God (Almighty)": 20x in 19 verses
4. by Whom? (Agent)	dual agents: Moses & Aaron [priests], Elijah & Elisha [prophets], Joshua & Zerubbabel: **2 lampstands & olive trees** ("sons of oil")	dual agents: 2 witnesses-prophets (combining roles) **2 lampstands & olive trees** [=faithful churches ("lampstands"): like Smyrna & Philadelphia?]
5. against Whom? (Target)	resistant Egyptians, rebellious N. Israel	"earth dwellers" judged (wrath), destroyers of the earth
6. for Whom? (Beneficiary)	Israel in Egypt, exilic & post-exilic Jews	servants, prophets, saints rewarded
7. How? (Means)	plagues, fire from God, rebuilt city & temple	oral "fire," plagues, death, abuse, exaltation

	Exodus, 1–2 Kings, Ezekiel, Zechariah	Revelation 11
9. Why/So What? (Point)	worship YHWH: Lord & King	Church: **worship** by all, **witness** by 2, **rule** by 1
10. Where? (Place)	[Sodom], Egypt, N. Kingdom, Babylon, Jerusalem	"Egypt & Sodom," the City where Lord crucified
	Jerusalem, **Temple**	Holy (heavenly?) *City* & **Temple**: altar & ark
11. How Much/Far? (Scope)	local	global
	ethnic	international
	particular	universal
	earthly	cosmic: visionary heaven & earth
12. When? (Time)	historical: Middle East	eschatological (between Jesus' 1st and 2nd comings)
	past & near future	future, "last" days

1. For another way of viewing this material, focusing more on the OT texts, rather than on their counterparts in Revelation 11, see the previous display (chart 16).

2. Whereas Ezekiel's hopes for the city and temple are oriented exclusively to the "not yet," would it be appropriate to regard John's vision as an expression of both "already" (in heaven) and "not yet" (upon the earth)?

18

Revelation 11 & 12: Two Facets of the Whole?

Chapter 11	Chapter 12
1. *Lord* was *crucified* (8)	*blood* of the *Lamb* (11)
2. two witnesses (3), **testimony** (7)	word of their **testimony** (11)
	hold the **testimony** of Jesus (17)
3. **loud voices in heaven** (15)	**loud voice in heaven** (10)
4. *has* become	now *have* come
5. **the kingdom of our** *Lord*	**the kingdom of our** *God*
6. **and of his Messiah**	**and the authority of his Messiah**
7. and he will *reign* forever / and begun to *reign* (17)	who is to *rule/shepherd* (5)
8. the kingdom of this world (15)	the nations

1. What do the close parallels in these two chapters suggest about their relationship?

2. In terms of order, did the events in chapter 11 chronologically precede those in chapter 12? Is this yet another indication that chronology and "linearity" are not a value for this author?

3. Which facet/side of the story does chapter 11 concentrate on?

4. What is the focus of chapter 12?

19

Dragon/Serpent Imagery: ANE & OT (Similarities)

	ANE: "Enuma Elish"	OT: Ps 74:12–17, 89:9–10
By Whom? (Agent)	Supreme God	Supreme God
What? (Event)	opposition/conflict: splitting watery carcass	opposition/conflict: dividing waters
Against Whom? (Target)	dragoness	Dragon–serpent
Where? (Place)	watery heavens ("literal")	water ("literal")
When? (Time)	primordial & creation of earth	primordial & creation of earth
Over What? (Significance)	Sovereignty, dominion, power	Sovereignty, dominion, power

1. See Foster for the text of "Enuma Elish." A water goddess Tiamat, represented as a dragon or serpent, defends her brood (minor deities) against attempts by senior deities to destroy them. A hero (Marduk) champions the latter on the condition that he become their head if victorious. After a ferocious battle, the victor slices her carcass longitudinally, creating from each half the heavens above and the earth below.

2. One need not come to hard and fast conclusions about the extent to which Israel borrowed or shared images and themes from its neighbors' literature. In either instance, that which was adopted was adapted in keeping with its authors' convictions about God. See differences (below) between and within.

20

Dragon/Serpent Imagery: ANE & OT (Differences)

	ANE: "Enuma Elish"	OT
By Whom? (Agent)	Supreme God: Marduk over others	Supreme and only God: of Israel, variously named
What? (Event)	opposition/conflict: splitting watery carcass	opposition/conflict: Exodus & Return from Exile
Against Whom? (Target)	dragoness/goddess & brood	Dragon: Pharaoh & Nabouchodonosor
Where? (Place)	watery heavens ("literal")	earthly water: R(e)ed Sea [and Euphrates]
When? (Time)	primordial	past, present, near future/eschaton
Over What? (Significance)	Sovereignty, dominion, power "above"	Sovereignty, dominion, power "below"

21

Dragon/Serpent Imagery: OT (Differences)

	(1)	(2)	(3)	(4)	(5)	(6)
	Ps 74:1–17	Ps 89:9–10	Isa 51:9–11	Isa 51:9–11	Ezek 29:2–5	Isa 27:1
What? (Event)	Creation: sun, lights, day, boundaries	Creation: earth's foundations, heavens	Redeemed crossing	Return from Exile	Hubris of Pharaoh	Finality
By Whom? (Agent)	God, king from of old	Lord God of Hosts	Yahweh	Yahweh	Yahweh	The Lord
Against Whom? (Object)	dragons, Leviathan	Rahab	Dragon, Rahab	Dragon, Rahab	Dragon, Pharaoh	Leviathan, dragon piercing serpent,
How? (Means)	slicing, dividing, breaking, cleaving	breaking, ruling, scattering, stilling waves	cutting, wounding, drying	cutting, wounding, drying	hooking	punishing, slaying
Where? (Place)	sea, waters	raging sea	sea [Nile River]	[Euphrates River]	Nile River	sea
When? (Time)	Past: "of old"	Primeval Past	Past	Future (near)	Future (near)	Future (distant?)
How Far? (Scope)	cosmic	cosmic	local	local	local	global, cosmic?

1. The link between dragon imagery and political rule(r) is clearly established in Ezekiel 29 (column 5). The location is specified, too: the Nile River. In LXX Jer 28:34–37, King Nabouchodonosor is regarded as a dragon about to devour Judah. During the century preceding Revelation, the Roman general Pompey, who had taken Jerusalem in 63 BCE, was likened to a dragon by the author of the Psalms of Solomon (2:20–(29)–35). See Charles and Charlesworth.

2. Why might the Egyptian pharaoh think that his *creation* of the Nile legitimates his *rule* over the land? Is the claim to god-like power over one realm being used to justify human sovereignty in the other?

3. On what basis does the author of Isaiah 51 (column 3) expect that God's people will be crossing another divided body of water (the Euphrates and Babylon's extensive canal system)?

4. Distinguish the various ways in which the common motif has been adapted to various episodes in the story of God's people. Should it come as any surprise that St. John might do the same?

5. Future references may be imminent, mid-range, and long-range in their proximity (columns 4–6). Ultimacy and finality (column 6) go hand in hand.

6. Is it true to say that issues of sovereignty, dominion, and power are at the heart of the struggle in every instance?

7. Is it significant that, in a "purely" creation text (column 1), God is referred to as "King . . . from of old"? Something similar is going on in Psalm 89, where the "Lord" God of "hosts/armies" is the divine appellation. Might the fact of opposition itself suggest a political contest?

22

Revelation 12 & Exodus Imagery

OT (Exodus 1, 4; 12–15 et al.)	Images of Revelation 12	Interpretation of Revelation 12
Israel: female image (Ezekiel 16, Hosea)	1) Woman	God's People (from whom Christ came)
Israel: son & king (Exod 4:22, 2 Sam 7:14–16)	2) Son	Jesus
Pharaoh-Dragon (Ezek 29:2–5)	3) Dragon	Devil/Satan/Herod/"caesars"
Pharaoh murdered boys	4) attempted murder of woman & her children	above enemies vs. Jesus & followers
released Israel	5) son to throne	Jesus' resurrection/ascension
pursued Israelites	6) pursued woman & children	pursued Jesus' followers
God's transport---eagle's wings (Exod 19:4)	7) eagle's wings	God's deliverance
Re(e)d Sea crossed	8) water from dragon's mouth	flood of satanic opposition
sea divided→dry ground	9) earth swallowed water	God's protection
Sinai desert	10) desert	wherever
physical food: manna & quail (Exodus 16)	11) divine nourishment	divine nourishment: spiritual food
	CATEGORIES	
"historical" narrative	12) Genre (Form?)	mythic narrative
salvation & establishment of Israel	13) Action (What?)	salvation & coming of God's Kingdom
God vs. human enemies	14) Agent/Target: Who(m)?	God vs. supernatural [and human] enemies
God for: ethnic & "national" Israel	14a) Agent/Beneficiary: Who(m)?	brothers & sisters, all who keep comm. & Jesus' witness
divine-human	15) Quality (What Kind?)	Divine-human-satanic
political-economic	15a) political-economic (including ch. 13)	political-economic [Cf. ch. 13]
Egypt	16) Place (Where?)	earth & heaven
local	17) Scope (How Far?)	global & cosmic

	CATEGORIES	
past/historical	18) **Time (When?)**	present ("now") & future/eschatological
divine (theocentric) intervention	19) **Means/Method (How?)**	by a "mere" angel, Lamb's death (theocentric christology), costly obedience
God rules thus rules over Egypt	20) **Significance (So What?)**	God thus rules over all: heaven, earth, cosmos

1. Although the "backgrounds" to chapter 12 include those of the Eastern Mediterranean and Mesopotamia in general (see chart 25), many of the terms and themes of this chapter can be found in the exodus event as recorded in the eponymous book and allied OT texts.

2. Both male and female images are applied to Israel, the former predominating, and, more often than not, exhibiting the role of the disobedient only son.

3. Is it fair to categorize John's use of his Scriptures as exhibiting a "rebirth of images" (the expression is Austin Farrer's)?

23

Revelation 12: "Satan's" Fall in Jewish Apocalyptic

1	2	3	4	5	6	7
Document, Date of composing	Isaiah 14 (8th–6th c. BCE)	Ezekiel 28 (6th c. BCE)	1 Enoch 6–16, Jubilees 5, 7, 10 (3rd–2nd c. BCE?)	Life of Adam & Eve 12–17 (1st c. BCE?)	2 Enoch 29:1–5 (1st c. BCE?)	Rev 12:1-11 (1st c. CE)
Who?	King of Babylon (human)	King of Tyre (human)	Angel-Semjaza	Angel	Angel	Dragon, Satan
What?	exalted his throne above stars, to be like the Most High; deposed	much trade → vast wealth → self-exaltation: "I am (a) God"; banished & destroyed	angels cohabit with women → giants → demons. Michael binds and ejects S. & angels	refuses to worship Adam, God's image; wants to supercede God; ejected with angels	attempts equality with God; ejected	attempts to devour new-born son who will rule the nations; overcome by Michael and angels; ejected
Where ?	from earth to sheol	"in Eden," on earth	from Heaven to darkness	from Heaven to earth	from Heaven to air above bottomless pit	from Heaven to earth
When?	Babylonian era	Tyrean era	prior to flood	creation of humans	creation of angels	Jesus' life, death, resurrection

47

1. Isaiah 14 (column 2) and Ezekiel 28 (column 3) unambiguously refer to the experiences of a human political figure: demotion resulting from hubris. In the case of the latter, vast political power and commercial wealth were the contributing factors. Regarding these personages as in any way supernatural is the result of injecting images and theology from later, non-canonical Jewish literature (columns 4-6).

2. In later centuries (more precise dating being problematic), these historical events were set in earlier eras: both prehistorical (columns 4–5) and primordial (column 6). It is here, in Jewish apocalyptic, that one first encounters the fall of a Satan-like figure. So far as canonical literature is concerned, the ejection of Satan from heaven is first recounted in Revelation 12.

3. The character of the protagonist changed as well: from human to supernatural, from angelic to satanic (columns 4–6).

4. So far as time is concerned, Revelation 12 is the only one of the above with an eschatological orientation relative to the others. However, John saw fulfillment as having occurred in his own immediate past: the Jesus event. Note especially the boundaries of vv. 5 and 11.

24
"I saw Satan fall from Heaven" (Luke 10:18)

	"I saw"	"Satan fall from heaven"
Long Ago?	Before the incarnation?	Before creation?
Recently?	During his lifetime?	At the temptation?

1. Did the Lukan Jesus (or the Jesus of the pre-Lukan tradition) claim in his pre-incarnate state to have observed a primordial event?

2. Did the "historical" Jesus of Luke (or the Jesus of the pre-Lukan tradition) claim to have seen an event occurring during his lifetime: e.g., following the temptation?

25

Myth in Revelation 12: Similarities*
Woman–Dragon–Child, War in Heaven

(1) Egyptian	(2) Greek	(3) Babylonian	(4) Jewish		(5) Christian (Rev 12:1–11)
Woman	**Woman**				**Woman**
Isis	Leto				(Israel?)
Pregnant	Pregnant				Pregnant
"mistress of Heaven"					Portent in Heaven
"Female sun"					Clothed with sun
Assoc. w. moon					Moon under feet
"Mistress of fate"					12-starred crown
Gives birth	Gives birth				Gives birth
Escapes	Escapes				Escapes
Protected	Protected & nourished				Protected & nourished
Dragon	**Dragon**				**Dragon**
Set-Typhon	Python				Serpent, Devil, Satan
Attacks her to	Attacks her to				Attacks her to
–destroy child	–destroy child				–destroy child
–retain kingship	–control oracle				–prevent rule
—over Eygpt	—& fate of nations				—over nations
Child	**Child**				**Child**
Horus	Apollo				God's Christ
—Escapes death	—Escapes death				—Escapes death
—Inherits throne	—Controls oracle				—taken to God & throne
	Dragon-Serpent	**Dragon**			**Dragon-Serpent**
	Typhon	Tiamat	Satanail		Devil, Satan

50

(1) Egyptian	(2) Greek	(3) Babylonian	(4) Jewish	(5) Christian (Rev 12:1–11)
	Heads-100	Heads-7		Heads-7
		(Red?)		Red
		Lifts tail		Tail swoops 1/3 stars
	Allies	Allies	Allies	Allies
	—Titans	—gods, demons	—angels	—stars/angels
	War in Heaven	War in Heaven	War in Heaven	War in Heaven
	Versus hero	Versus hero	Versus hero	Versus hero
	—Zeus	—Marduk	—God-Michael	—Michael
	Over rule	Over rule	Over rule	Over rule
	Defeat –expulsion	Defeat-expulsion	Defeat-expulsion	Defeat-expulsion
	–to netherworld	–to netherworld	–to netherworld	
	—Tartarus		—earth	—to earth
			—above abyss	

*This should be examined in relation to chart 26. "Myth in Revelation 12: Contrasts."

1. For the primary sources underlying this display and the next, see Budge, Charles, Charlesworth, Foster, Grant, and Most. Important secondary sources include Aune, A. Y. Collins, Fontenrose, Ions, and MacKenzie.

2. A Woman-Child-Dragon/Serpent myth (column 2) had circulated among the Greeks and Egyptians: Zeus (the Greek high god) had impregnated Leto (a mortal). Python, a huge dragon/snake, who feared losing control of a prophetic oracle that foretold (and so controlled) the destiny of nations, tried to eliminate the threat from her unborn son, Apollo, by attempting to devour both. However, she escaped to a place of refuge—from which her son returned to conquer the serpent and gain control of the oracle (Grant). (See why the dragon/serpent/Devil/Satan wished to devour the child in Rev 12:5). The Egyptians (column 1) had their version of this theme: Typhon/Set vs. Isis and Horus (Budge).

3. See modern reflections on the Woman-Child-Dragon motif in the writings of D. H. Lawrence and C. G. Jung.

4. The uprising of one group of gods against another for control led by a dragon/serpent figure (columns 2 and 3) also circulated among Babylonians (Marduk vs. Tiamat, chart 20) and Greeks (clash of the Titans),

resulting in the vanquished being hurled to earth or some other nether region (Foster and Most). Note those OT writers who turned the myth into metaphors in accounts of "historical" events.

5. For the intertestamental/Second Temple apocalyptic Jewish texts, see columns 4–6 of chart 23 on " 'Satan's' Fall." The three accounts vary regarding the time and occasion of this conflict: just before the flood, after the creation of Adam, and on the second day of creation (that which column 4, above, recounts). The same may be said for Jewish appropriation of the War in Heaven myth as was suggested regarding the OT's use of the Yahweh vs. the Dragon myth.

6. It is here, in Jewish apocalyptic, that one first encounters the fall of a Satan-like figure. However, so far as canonical literature is concerned, the ejection of the devil from heaven is first recounted in Revelation 12.

7. Furthermore, so far as I am aware, Revelation 12 represents the first time in all of ancient literature that the Woman-Child-Dragon/Serpent and War in Heaven motifs (whether in whole or in part is debated) have been brought together in a single passage. With what event is the latter connected, positioned as it is between vv. 5 and 11? How does this fit with common notions within and outside of the church?

8. Although critical scholars have to greater or lesser extents addressed these phenomena (especially Aune and A. Y. Collins), the data thus displayed visually (and uniquely, so far as I can tell) convey how much the myths impacted John's imagination and theologizing.

9. Given the political element found in combat myths and metaphors, might the reptilian references include human agents as well as supernatural ones? Because of Isa 27:1, is it necessary to identify "that ancient serpent" (Rev 12:9) with Genesis 3 (where Satan is not actually mentioned)?

26

Myth in Revelation 12: Differences*
Woman-Child-Dragon

	Greece	Revelation 12:1–11	Egypt
1. Against Whom-1? (Female)	Leto (individual)	People of God (collective)	Isis (individual)
2. Against Whom-2? (Child)	Apollo	child/son [=Jesus]	Horus
3. By Whom? (Dragon Figure)	Python	Dragon/Serpent/ Satan/Devil	Set-Typhon
4. Where? (Place-1)	Parnasus, Greece	Calvary-Jerusalem	Egypt
5. Where? (Place-2)	Delos	God's throne	throne of Egypt
6. How? (Means of Victory)	overwhelming conventional force (arrows)	blood of the Lamb, witness of brothers and sisters	
7. When? (Time)	primordial/distant past	recent past	primordial/ distant past
8. Genre? (Form)	myth	"historicized" myth	myth

*This should be examined in relation to Chart 25. "Myth in Revelation 12: Similarities."

1. Although many Roman Catholic scholars interpret the woman of Revelation 12 (line 1) as Mary, and thus an individual, why is there a tendency among most others to view her in collective terms? Would you be surprised were it to be discovered that Leto and Isis "embodied" collectives (the people/nation) in themselves—as royal/political figures tend to do?

2. What difference(s) from the others does the array of names given to the antagonist in chapter 12 suggest?

3. Leto, Apollo, and Python are terrestrial figures—the woman, child, and dragon being celestial. However, is there any evidence that the child might be "grounded," too?

4. Although the reason for the conflict (the **Why?**) is the same (over who will rule), what of the means of victory (**How?** line 6)? What role does the witness borne by the brothers and sisters play?

5. Since some of the dragon imagery in the prophetic passages in charts 19–21 had been applied to reigning kings, might there be at least a partial, indirect political reference here, too?

6. Thanks go to my colleagues, Steve Perisho and Albert Ferreiro, for helping me to find a version of an ancient Latin Christian hymn, whose author I had supposed was Aurelius Clemens Prudentius (348–403 [?] CE). According to my memory, the text had read, "Thou hast conquered, O True Apollo: Thou hast vanquished the Python of hell." However, after I had failed to locate the source and actual text, they pointed me to a verse by Paulinus of Nola (a near contemporary of Prudentius): "Hail, O true Apollo! Renowned Healer! / Victor over the dragon of hell! / . . . Glorious in thy triumph! / Hail thou happy victory of this age! / Parent of the blessed days to come!" "Salve, O Apollo vere, Paean inclite, / Pulsor draconis inferi! / . . . [lines 51–52]. Io triumphe [or, "In triumpho"] nobilis! / Salve beata saeculi victoria, / Parens beati temporis!" [lines 60-62] (de Hartel).

7. Would the author have seen any reason to pit "Jerusalem" against "Athens"? Do we have here a profound expression of that which Arthur Holmes popularized: "All Truth is God's Truth"? Could we say that all true myth is God's myth? Among conservative Christians (some of them evangelicals), the positive appropriation of myth has been championed by Fuller, Lewis, Markos, Tolkien, and Yancey.

8. Would you agree with Lewis, who spoke about the truth of myth, that this was an instance of "Myth Became Fact"? If not, might one go so far as to say that, in Revelation 12, myth became historicized (as it had in some of the prophetic texts examined in charts 19–21), given the time and place?

27

Revelation 12: The Kerygma/Gospel-in-Myth

Unifying Kerygma of the NT	Revelation 12
1. God who	God ["divine passive"] (5)
2. raised	took up to throne
3. Jesus	son/child
4. a response	keep commands, hold testimony (17)
5. towards God	of God, of Jesus
6. brings benefits	overcame Dragon/Serpent/Satan/Devil (11)
	—by the Lamb's blood

1. I have shown (in "The Unifying Kerygma of the New Testament") that Revelation 12 is one of nineteen instances among the twenty-seven books of the NT that reflect the unifying kerygma (Gospel announcement) of the NT. The standard elements of this kerygmatic "form" do not always appear in a rigid sequence. Rather, they belong to an informal formality.

2. As in other NT literature, but here more dramatically, the pattern is embedded in a particular genre and a specific application. In Revelation, that genre is myth. In the language of the Theologian, the content was being conveyed in two "great signs" (vv. 1 and 3). This is the mode, announced early on (1:1) but obscured in nearly every translation, by which he would be articulating the entire message.

3. By appropriating canonical Scriptures, allied Jewish texts (of varying authority), and the great myths of Mediterranean and Mesopotamian culture, this fisher of men and women cast his net more widely than any theologian-evangelist before or after him had done or would do.

28

Revelation 12 & Matthew 1–2: Two "Christmas Stories"

Revelation 12	Matthew 1-2
1. Woman [Israel]	Woman (Mary)
2. Pregnant	Pregnant
3. Child/newborn son	Child/newborn son: Jesus
4. Great Red Dragon (Cf. Ezek 29:3, 32:2)	King Herod
5. Attempts to devour child	Attempts to kill Jesus
6. Who will rule/be king of the nations?	Who is king of the Jews?
7. (Latin: "Gentes" = nations/Gentiles)	Magi from the East worship Jesus as king
8. Child is taken up to God's throne	
9. Woman flees to desert	Holy Family flees to Egypt [through desert]
10. Dragon pursues woman	Herod seeks to destroy Jesus
11. Dragon wars on rest of offspring	Herod kills male children

1. As in the case of Revelation, so it is in Matthew. The issue is political: who will be king/rule? The first gospel begins with Jesus' genealogy; the second two-thirds lists Jesus' royal heritage. Relate the political ter-

Revelation 12 & Matthew 1–2: Two "Christmas Stories"

minology of Revelation to the central subject of Jesus' preaching and teaching in all three synoptic Gospels: the kingdom of heaven/God. The true King of the Jews cast out demons, who were under satan's/dragon's control. See especially the parable of the strong(er) man: Matt 12:22–30, Mark 3:22–27, and Luke 11:14–20. Each in his own way (gospel narrative and apocalyptic vision) portrays the titanic struggle for power that accompanied Jesus' appearance.

2. King Herod becomes the most recent political figure embodying (or worthy of being compared with) the dragon/serpent—like the Egyptian Pharaoh (Ezek 29:2–3); the Babylonian Nabouchodonosor (LXX Jeremiah 28:34); and, most recently (by inference from the context), the Roman general, Pompey, who had captured Jerusalem (Pss Sol 2:25) in 63 BCE.

3. In both instances, God's rule upsets worldly notions of power. The question always being addressed is, "Who rules—and how"? Not the great red dragon, but the vulnerable newborn and the slaughtered lamb (Rev 12:5, 11), not the authority represented by Herod and Rome, but by the willing sacrifice of Jesus (Matt 26:27–29).

29

Revelation 13–14: Animal Imagery & Followers Contrasted

Followers			Animals	
		Beast		Lamb
	description	ch. 13		ch. 14
	destiny	ch. 14		ch. 14

1. Do opposing animalistic images help to relate the two chapters?

2. Common to each is a description and destiny of their respective followers, which are contrasted as well.

30

Revelation 13 & 14: Sinners & Saints Contrasted (by Chiasmus?)

```
 a    b    b'   a'
(13) (13) (14) (14)
```

	Chapter 13		Chapter 14	
	marked by beast		name of Father & Lamb	
(A) Sinners	follow beast		144K follow Lamb	Saints (B')
	worship beast		sing [worship]	
	attacked		[ignore Gospel]	
(B) Saints	conquered		"harvested"	Sinners (A')
	killed		tormented	

1. Another way of relating chapters 13 and 14 is to focus on the contrasting characteristics or experiences of the followers, here designated for the sake of alliteration as "sinners" and "saints."

2. Yet again, chiasmus reverses the sequence of each. In chapter 13, consideration of sinners precedes that of the saints. In chapter 14, the reverse is true: saints come before sinners.

31

The Beasts of Revelation 13: A Summary of Interpretive Tendencies*

	(1)	(2)	(3)	(4)
	Ancient/Historical	On-going	Contemporary	Eschatological
Perspective	preterist	idealist/spiritualist	=	futurist
Time	past	always	interpreter's present	future
Millennialism	pre-	a-	=	pre-
Church		+/-	popes/papacy	+/-
			institution / hierarchy	+/-
			(by Roman Catholics	
			& Protestants)	
World (Politics, Religion, Movements)	+	+/-	Islam, UN, EU, gurus,	=
			big gov't, -isms, etc.	=
Individual (soul, internal)		+	+/-	

*This chart summarizes and tabulates the discussion of Kovacs and Rowland throughout their jointly-authored work.

1. Column 1 includes those who take the preterist perspective on Revelation; that is, so far as **Time** is concerned, both beastly figures refer to political leaders who functioned during the first century in the Mediterranean **World** of the Roman Empire. The earliest **Millennial** view

of which we are aware seems to have posited Jesus' return as occurring prior to his one thousand year reign (pre-millennial). Predictive prophecy would have been of the short-range variety.

2. Those who view Revelation as addressing **On-going** issues (column 2) that always confront readers throughout time (idealist/spiritualist), belong to the a-millennial persuasion. In a book so full of symbols, why literalize numbers? Thus, the millennium refers to the entire period (inclusive of both successes and failures) between Jesus' first and second appearances. Opinion is divided (+/-) as to whether the beasts refer to leaders "out" in the world or within the **Church**. At the very least, whatever is happening "externally" in either of the two spheres, **Individuals** can experience the struggles and victories between warring factions within the soul.

3. Another version of the former orientation (and perspective) belongs to those interpreters who see the events of Revelation taking place in their **Contemporary** situation (column 3). Thus, some medieval readers within the Roman Catholic **Church** (in their own "now") viewed one or more popes (or the ecclesial hierarchy) as tools of the evil one. Certain sixteenth-century reformers joined that chorus! Others have seen/do see the threat as coming from one's external context in the **World**: the rise of Islam, various political figures and institutions, and the competing "–isms" vying for adherents in the public square. In addition to or apart from such collective dimensions, some restrict themselves to the more private, internal, and **Individual** sphere of operation.

4. So far as **Eschatology** is concerned (column 4), the futurist concentrates on the end-**Time**. He or she will be a pre-millennialist. Thus, whether arising internally from the **Church** or externally from the **World**, beasts one and two are yet to come. The returning Jesus will put an end to these agents of the devil/Satan, after which he reigns together with his saints. St. John's predictions are thought to have been of the long-range variety—most of the beasts' activities taking place shortly before and immediately after Jesus' second coming. Although not prohibiting an internal, **Individual** appropriation of this message, proponents stress the **Church** and **World** as the stages upon which the political and ecclesial drama will occur.

32

Revelation 17–18: The Prostitute, Babylon, Beasts, & Kings (Their Relationships)

	Great Britain (merely illustrative!)	Babylon (Revelation 17)
1. Female Symbol	Britannia	Prostitute
2. Political System	British Empire	Babylon
3. System's Rulers	Royal Family (the State Dynasty) Her Majesty's Governments Prime Minster, Parliament	Beast(s)
4. Local Rulers	local kings	kings
"Rome is an Idea."*	"Great Britain is an Idea."	"Babylon is an Idea."

*See chart 34 for an account of this statement's origin and application.

Among the interpretive challenges in chapters 17–18 is to relate the various political images and personages to one another. The above attempts to do so with the realization that, in the experience of visions and dreams, categories are fluid and are subject to a good deal of overlapping. One could just as easily substitute "Columbia" as the female image for the United States. However, it is less familiar than "Britannia," even in the Americas. And delimiting the boundaries of an American "Empire" would be harder to do.

33

Revelation 17–19: Babylon & New Jerusalem

1. City (human community)	Babylon (Revelation 17–18)	New Jerusalem (Revelation 19)
2. Animal Image/Logo	Beast	Lamb
3. Role	Prostitute	Bride/Wife
4. Clothes	purple, scarlet	white (19:8)
5. Accessories	jewels, gold, pearls	materials of the city (20)
6. Character	unfaithful, for sale	faithful to husband (Lamb)

34

Revelation 17–21: History, Myth, & Eschatology

+Babylon & Jerusalem	Historic	Mythic*	Eschatological
	was	is	will be
1. Time	past	present	future
	then	now	eternal: New Jerusalem (NJ)
	once	once and on-going	forever: (NJ)
2. Place	earth	earth	New Earth
3. Scope	local (Middle East)	global	cosmic: "above" & "below" (NJ)
4. Focus	particular	universal	universal
5. Perspective	preterist	idealist/spiritualist	all
+Supply "Rome," etc.		*i.e., foundational	

1. In the film, *Gladiator*, the emperor says to the hero Maximus, "Rome is an Idea"—and a collective one at that. Indeed, the city, republic, and empire had boundaries, buildings, roads, leaders, the army, and institutions (civic, cultural, commercial, and religious). However, Rome first became embedded in and emanated from the minds of patricians and plebeians alike. So it is with Babylon and (New) Jerusalem. These are two views of power and two strategies (politics: human vs. divine) for distributing it within communities.

2. Do you sense a note of regret expressed in Revelation 18 that Babylon had not become all that she could have been? Does the repentance of Nebuchadnezzar King of Babylon (Daniel 4), who had destroyed the Kingdom of Judah and taken the upper echelons of politics, commerce, and society into exile, suggest a wideness of God's mercy that might be applied in the future?

3. Only two qualities of life are possible for humans living in community: Babylon, ascendant (resulting in hubris, oppression, and downfall) or New Jerusalem, descendant (resulting in humility, service, and exaltation).

35

Revelation 17, 19, 21

A Tale of Two Cities? of Two Women?

Babylon: Woman (Whore)—City (17:4)	New Jerusalem: City (21:1, 15-21)—Woman (Bride) 19:8, 21:2
1. purple & scarlet	1. fine linen, bright & clean (=righteous deeds, 19:8)
2. gold	2. gold: wall & city
3. precious stones	3. precious stones; jewels: jasper, sapphire, agate
4. pearls	4. pearls

1. Are the city's plan and materials, in the case of the New Jerusalem, to be understood any more literally than the women and their apparel in each case? What is the reality in each instance?

2. Does the author himself provide a more direct clue in the interpretation that he supplies at 19:8?

3. Consider the picture of a city with both high walls (security) and many gates (access)—all of which are open 24/7. Could both be achieved simultaneously in a conventional "city"?

4. Might these images speak more about people in community than materials and structures?

Bibliography

Aune, David. *Revelation 6-16*. Word Biblical Commentary 52b. Nashville: Thomas Nelson, 1968. Pages 667-74.
Bowker, John. "The Son of Man." *JTS* 28 (1977) 19-48.
Budge, E. A. Wallis. *Legends of the Gods: The Egyptian Texts*. London: Kegan Paul, Trench and Trübner, 1912. Pages 142-44.
Burkett, Delbert. *The Son of Man Debate: A History and Evaluation*. SNTSMS 107. Cambridge: Cambridge University Press, 1999. Pages 13-21, esp. 14-17.
Caird, George B. "The Language of Eschatology." In *The Language and Imagery of the Bible*. Philadelphia: Westminster, 1980. Pages 243-71.
———. "The Language of Myth." In *The Language and Imagery of the Bible*. Philadelphia: Westminster, 1980. Pages 219-42.
Charles, R. H. *Apocrypha and Pseudepigrapha of the Old Testament*. Vol. 2. Oxford: Clarendon, 1913. Pages 633-34.
Collins, Adela Yarbro. *The Combat Myth in the Book of Revelation*. Eugene, OR: Wipf and Stock, 2001.
Collins, John J. *Daniel: A Commentary on the Book of Daniel*. Hermeneia: A Critical and Historical Commentary on the Bible. Minneapolis: Fortress, 1993. Pages 308-10, 317-18.
Conkle, Nancy. *The Ancient Near East: A Bellerophon Coloring Book*. Santa Barbara, CA: Bellerophon, 1968.
Dessenne, A. *Le Sphinx; étude iconographique*. Edited by E. de Boccard. Bibliothèque des Écoles Françaises d' Athenès et de Rome 186. Paris: E. de Boccard, 1957. Plate 28, fig. 226.
Farrer, Austin. *A Rebirth of Images: The Making of St. John's Apocalypse*. Philadelphia: Westminster, Dacre, 1949.
Fontenrose, Joseph Eddy. *Python: A Study of Delphic Myth and Its Origins*. Berkeley: University of California Press, 1959. Pages 1-27.
Foster, Benjamin R. "Enuma Elish" in *The Context of Scripture*, edited by William W. Hallo. Vol. 1. New York: Brill, 1997. Tablets 1-5, pp. 390-400.
Fuller, Edmund, et al. *Myth, allegory, and gospel: An Interpretation of J. R. R. Tolkien, C. S. Lewis, G. K. Chesterton, and Charles Williams*. Minneapolis: Bethany Fellowship, 1974.
Hassan, Selim. *The Sphinx: Its History in the Light of Recent Excavations*. Cairo: Government Press, 1949. Pages 112-13.
Hogarth, D. G. *Carchemish: Report on the Excavations at Djerabis on Behalf of the British Museum* vol. 1. London: British Museum, 1914.
Hyginus, C. Julius. "Fabulae" in *The Myths of Hyginus*. Translated and edited by Mary Grant. Lawrence: University of Kansas Press, 1960. Page 140.
Ions, Veronica. *Egyptian Mythology*. New York: Bedrick, 1983. Pages 56-67.

Jung, Carl Gustav. "Answer to Job," in *Collected Works*. Edited by H. Read et al. Translated by R. F. C. Hull. Vol. 11; Bollingen Series XX; sec. ed.; Princeton, NJ: University Press, 1969. Pages 438–44.

Kim, Seyoon. *"The 'Son of Man'" as the Son of God*. Grand Rapids: Eerdmans, 1983. Pages 25, 36.

Kovacs, Judith and Christopher Rowland. *Revelation*. Oxford: Blackwell, 2004.

Lawrence, D. H. "The Dragon of the Apocalypse" in *Selected Literary Criticism*, edited by Anthony Beal; New York: Viking, 1956. Pages 153–66.

Lemcio, Eugene E. "'Son of Man,' 'Pitiable Man,' 'Rejected Man': Equivalent Expressions in the Old Greek of Daniel," *TynBul* 56.1 (2005) 43–60.

———. "The Unifying Kerygma of the New Testament," Appendix in *The Past of Jesus in the Gospels*. SNTSMS 69. New York: Cambridge University Press, 1991. Pages 115–31 and 158–62. This appendix combines and expands the results from two earlier articles of the same title, in *JSNT* 33 (1988) 3–17 and (as Part II) in *JSNT* 38 (1990) 3–11. In the monograph, a chart displays the texts at a glance, and an excursus shows the pattern persisting into the sub-Apostolic period.

Lewis, C. S. "Myth Became Fact." In *God in the Dock: Essays on Theology and Ethics*, edited by Walter Hooper. Grand Rapids: Eerdmans, 1970. Pages 63–67.

MacKenzie, Donald. *Egyptian Myth and Legend*. New York: Bell, 1978.

Markos, Louis A. "Myth Matters," *CT* (April 23, 2001) 32–39.

Most, Glenn W., ed. *Hesiod: Theogony, Works and Days, Testimonia*. LCL. Cambridge, MA: Harvard University Press, 2006. Lines 617–72, 820–69 (52–56, 68–72).

Moule, C. F. D. *The Origin of Christology*. New York: Cambridge University Press, 1977. Pages 11–22.

Paulinus of Nola. "Carmen II." In *S. Pontii Meropii Paulini Nolani Opera*, edited by Willhelm de Hartel, 348–50. Corpus scriptorum ecclesiasticorum latinorum 30. Prague: F. Tempsky, 1894.

Pietersma, Albert, and Benjamin G. Wright, eds. *A New English Translation of the Septuagint*. New York: Oxford University Press, 2007.

Pritchard, James B., ed. *Ancient Near Eastern Texts Relating to the Old Testament*. 3rd ed. Princeton, NJ: Princeton University Press, 1969. Pages 61–63, 67.

Rahner, Hugo. *Greek Myths and Christian Mystery*. New York: Harper and Row, 1963. Page 122.

Rowland, Christopher. *The Open Heaven: A Study of Apocalyptic in Judaism and Early Christianity*. New York: Crossroad, 1982. Pages 100–101, 178–83.

Traina, Robert A. *Methodical Bible Study: A New Approach to Hermeneutics*. New York: Biblical Seminary in New York, 1952.

Wall, Robert W. *Revelation*. New International biblical commentary 18. Peabody, MA: Hendrickson, 1991.

Wilson, Mark. *Charts on the Book of Revelation: Literary, Historical, and Theological Perspectives*. Grand Rapids: Kregel, 2007.

Woolley, Leonard. *Carchemish: Report on the Excavations at Jerablus on Behalf of the British Museum*. vol. 3; London: British Museum, 1952.

Wright, R. B., ed. "Psalms of Solomon" in *The Old Testament Pseudepigrapha: Expansions of the "Old Testament" and Legends, Wisdom and Philosophical Literature, Prayers, Psalms and Odes, Fragments of Lost Judeo-Hellenistic Works*, edited by James H. Charlesworth, vol. 2; New York: Doubleday, 1985. Page 653 n. a2.

Yancey, Philip. "Cosmic Combat." *Christianity Today* (December 12, 1994) 20–23.

www.ingramcontent.com/pod-product-compliance
Lightning Source LLC
Chambersburg PA
CBHW070109100426
42743CB00012B/2702